Eccles Surname

Ireland: 1600s to 1900s

From Ireland Church Records of Baptism, Marriage and Death

Comprised of Roman Catholic and Church of Ireland Records

From Counties Carlow, Cork, Kerry and Dublin City

Compiled by **Donovan Hurst**

March 14, 2012

ISBN: 0985134380
ISBN-13: 978-0-9851343-8-9

Dedication

This work is dedicated to all of those that came before us and shaped our lives to make us the people that we are today.

Table of Contents

Introduction

This is a compilation of individuals who have the surname of Eccles that lived in the country of Ireland from the 1600s to the 1900s. I have placed each entry into one of four categories: Families, Individual Births/Baptisms, Individual Burials, and Individual Marriages. If a marriage entry primarily concerns an Individual Eccles who is female, then I have placed that entry under the category of Individual Marriages. If a marriage entry primarily concerns an Individual Eccles who is male, then I have placed that entry under the category of Families. Images of many of these listings are available at http://churchrecords.irishgenealogy.ie/churchrecords/.

To help guide the reader of this work, the format of this book is as follows:

- Main Family Entry (Husband and Wife) (Father and Mother)

  - Child of Main Family Entry, including Spouse(s) when available

    - Grandchild of Main Family Entry, including Spouse(s) when available

      - Great-Grandchild of Main Family Entry, including Spouse(s) when available

(**Bolded Text**) following any entry includes any additional information such as Residence(s), Occupation(s), Signature(s), etc. when available.

Hurst

Some of the fonts used in this work symbolizes Celtic writing. The traditional letters, numbers, and punctuation marks and their Celtic counterparts are as follows:

Traditional Letters (Uppercase & Lowercase)

A a B b C c D d E f G g H h I i J j K k L l M m N n O o P p Q q R r S s T t U u V v W w X x Y y Z z

Celtic Letters (Uppercase & Lowercase)

A a B b C c D ð E e F ꝼ G g H ḣ I í J j K k L l M m

N n O o P p Q q R ʀ S s T t U u V u W ɯ X x Y ʏ Z z

Traditional Numbers

1 2 3 4 5 6 7 8 9 10

Celtic Numbers

1 2 3 4 5 6 7 8 9 10

Traditional Punctuation

. , : ' " & - ( )

Celtic Punctuation

. , : ' " & - ( )

Parish Churches

Cork & Ross

(Roman Catholic or RC)

Bantry Parish, Cork - SS. Peter & Paul Parish, Rossalettiri & Kilkeraunmor (Roscarbery & Lissevard) Parish, and Skibbereen (Creagh & Sullon) Parish.

Dublin (Church of Ireland)

Leeson Park Parish, Sandford Parish, St. Anne Parish, St. Audoen Parish, St. Catherine Parish, St. George Parish, St. James Parish, St. John Parish, St. Mark Parish, St. Mary Parish, St. Michael Parish, St. Michan Parish, St. Nicholas Within Parish, St. Nicholas Without Parish, St. Patrick Parish, St. Paul Parish, St. Peter Parish, St. Stephen Parish, St. Thomas Parish, and St. Werburgh Parish.

Dublin (Roman Catholic or RC)

Saggart Parish, SS. Michael & John Parish, St. Agatha Parish, St. Andrew Parish, St. Audoen Parish, St. James Parish, St. Lawrence Parish, St. Mary, Pro Cathedral Parish, St. Michan Parish, and St. Nicholas Parish.

Kerry (Roman Catholic or RC)

Glengarriff Parish.

Families

- Arthur Eccles & Sarah Pogue – 3 Aug 1725 (Marriage, **St. Nicholas Within Parish**)

- Charles Eccles & Isabel Unknown

  o John Stewart Eccles, b. 6 Oct 1847, bapt. 4 Nov 1847 (Baptism, **St. Peter Parish**) & Caroline Frances

     Browne – 23 May 1871 (Marriage, **St. Stephen Parish**)

Signatures:

   ▪ Amy Henrietta Frances Eccles, b. 22 Apr 1874, bapt. 13 May 1874 (Baptism, **St. Anne Parish**) &

      John Knox McClintock – 27 Apr 1893 (Marriage, **St. Stephen Parish**)

Signatures:

Amy Henrietta Frances Eccles (daughter):

   Residence - Eccles Ville, Fintona, Co. Tyrone - April 27, 1893

   Relationship Status at Marriage - minor

John Knox McClintock, son of George Perry McClintock (son-in-law):

   Residence - Seskinare, Omagh, Co. Tyrone - April 27, 1893

   Occupation - Captain, Tyrone Militia - April 27, 1893

George Perry McClintock (father):

Occupation - Colonel in the Militia

John Stewart Eccles (father):

Occupation - Esquire

Wedding Witnesses:

W. G. Brooke & Augustus McClintock

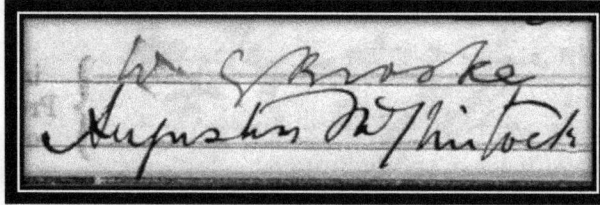

Signatures:

- Rose Isabel De Montmormey (M o n t m o r m e y) Eccles – b. 5 Jan 1876, bapt. 2 Feb 1876 (Baptism,

  St. Peter Parish)

- Anne Theodosia Hester Eccles – b. 9 Feb 1878, bapt. 7 Mar 1878 (Baptism, **St. Peter Parish**)

John Stewart Eccles (son):

Residence - Eccles Ville, Co. Tyrone - May 23, 1871

Eccles Ville, Co. Tyrone - February 2, 1876

March 7, 1878

Eccles Ville, Fintona - May 13, 1874

22 Lower Fitzwilliam Street - May 23, 1871

8 Leinster Street, Dublin - May 13, 1874

March 7, 1878

33 Lower Lesson Street - February 2, 1876

Occupation - Esquire - May 23, 1871

February 2, 1876

D. L. - March 7, 1878

Caroline Browne, daughter of Thomas Richardson Browne (daughter-in-law):

Residence - 8 Leinster Street - May 23, 1871

Eccles Surname Ireland: 1600s to 1900s

Thomas Richardson Browne (father):

Signature:

  Occupation - D. L.

Charles Eccles (father):

  Occupation - D. L.

Wedding Witnesses:

Thomas Richardson Browne & Charles E. Eccles

Signatures:

  o   Anne Henrietta Eccles, b. 28 Jan 1849, bapt. 19 Feb 1849 (Baptism, **St. Peter Parish**) & Conolly

      William Lecky Browne – 28 Nov 1878 (Marriage, **St. Anne Parish**)

Signature:

Signatures (Marriage):

Anne Henrietta Eccles (daughter):

Residence - Eccles Ville, Fentown, Co. Tyrone - November 28, 1878

Connolly William Lecky Browne, son of Thomas Richardson Browne (son-in-law):

Residence - Shelbourne Hotel - November 28, 1878

Aughentaine Castle, Five Miletown, Co. Tyrone - November 28, 1878

Occupation - Esquire - November 28, 1878

Thomas Richardson Browne (father):

Signature:

Occupation - Esquire

Charles Eccles (father):

Occupation - Esquire

Wedding Witnesses:

Charles E. Eccles & Theodosia Browne

Signatures:

Eccles Surname Ireland: 1600s to 1900s

o   Charles Edward Eccles, b. 20 Oct 1850, bapt. 14 Nov 1850 (Baptism, **St. Peter Parish**) & Matilda

Theodosia Browne – 11 Dec 1883 (Marriage, **St. Anne Parish**)

Signatures:

Signatures (Marriage):

Charles Edward Eccles (son):

  Residence - Rochfort Lodge, Bundoran, Co. Down - December 11, 1883

  Occupation - Captain Royal Artillery - December 11, 1883

Matilda Theodosia Browne, daughter of Thomas Richardson Browne (daughter-in-law):

  Residence - Fintimara, Warren Point, Co. Down - December 11, 1883

Hurst

Thomas Richardson Browne (father):

Signature:

    Occupation - Esquire

Charles Eccles (father):

    Occupation - Esquire

Wedding Witnesses:

Connolly William Lecky Browne & Rose Sarah Browne

Signatures:

- o   Constance Isabel Eccles & James Vesey Lendrum – 28 Nov 1885 (Marriage, **St. Anne Parish**)

Signatures:

Constance Isabel Eccles (daughter):

    Residence - Eccles Ville, Fintona, Co. Tyrone - November 28, 1885

James Vesey Lendrum, son of James Lendrum (son-in-law):

    Residence - The United Service Club, Dublin - November 28, 1885

        Derrybard, Omagh - November 28, 1885

    Occupation - Captain Seaforth Highlanders - November 28, 1885

James Lendrum (father):

    Occupation - D L

Charles Eccles (father):

    Occupation - D L

Wedding Witnesses:

Unknown Major of the Seaforth Highlanders & Charles E. Eccles Captain Royal Artillery

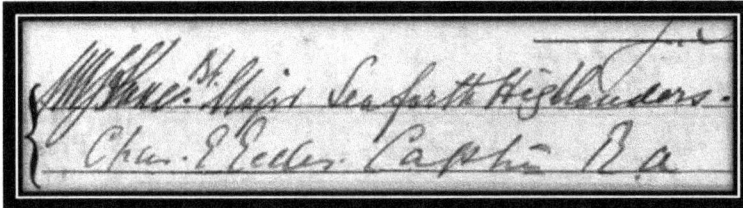

Signatures:

    o   Robert Gilbert Eccles – b. 25 Oct 1854, bapt. 8 Nov 1854 (Baptism, **St. Peter Parish**)

Charles Eccles (father):

    Residence - Fintona, Co. Sefrone - November 4, 1847

                            November 14, 1850

        36 Upper Fitzwilliam Street - February 19, 1849

         8 Upper Fitzwilliam Street - November 8, 1854

    Occupation - Gentleman - November 4, 1847

               Esquire - February 19, 1849

                    November 14, 1850

                    November 8, 1854

Hurst

- Charles Eccles & Mary Foy – 18 Jul 1826 (Marriage, **St. Andrew Parish** (RC))

  - Alice Eccles – bapt. 1827 (Baptism, **St. Andrew Parish** (RC))

  - Thomas Eccles – bapt. 1828 (Baptism, **St. Andrew Parish** (RC))

  - Margaret Eccles – bapt. 1832 (Baptism, **St. Andrew Parish** (RC))

  - Charles Eccles – bapt. 1834 (Baptism, **St. Andrew Parish** (RC))

  - Margaret Eccles – bapt. 1838 (Baptism, **St. Andrew Parish** (RC))

  - Mary Anne Eccles – bapt. 1840 (Baptism, **St. Andrew Parish** (RC))

  - Patrick Eccles – bapt. 1843 (Baptism, **St. Andrew Parish** (RC))

- Charles Eccles & Rebecca Stewart – 11 Jul 1745 (Marriage, **St. Michan Parish**)

Charles Eccles (husband):

Occupation - Esquire - July 11, 1745

- Christopher Eccles & Celia Eccles

  - Christopher Eccles – b. 1 Jan 1854, bapt. 11 Jan 1854 (Baptism, **St. Mary, Pro Cathedral Parish** (RC))

Christopher Eccles (father):

Residence - 5 Henry Street - January 11, 1854

Eccles Surname Ireland: 1600s to 1900s

- Cuthbert Eccles & Catherine Thomas – 30 Apr 1819 (Baptism, **St. George Parish**)

Signature:

Signature (Marriage):

- Henry Eccles – b. 4 May 1820, bapt. 18 Sep 1821 (Baptism, **St. George Parish**)

- John Eccles, b. 6 May 1820, bapt. 18 Sep 1821 (Baptism, **St. George Parish**) & Harriet Frizell – 2

  Aug 1854 (Marriage, **St. Peter Parish**)

Signature:

Signatures (Marriages):

9

- Ellen Harriet Eccles & Montague Maxwell Carpendale – 13 Sep 1882 (Marriage, **Leeson Park Parish**)

Signatures:

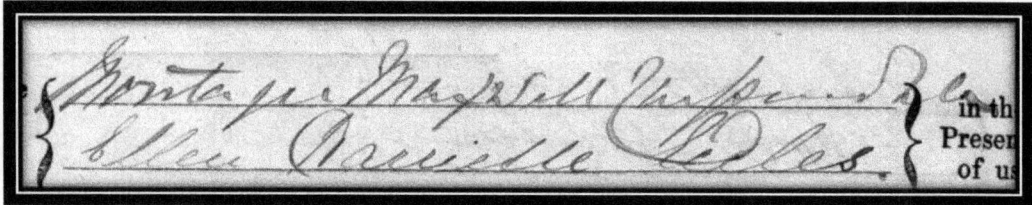

Ellen Harriet Eccles (daughter):

Residence - Drogheda - September 13, 1882

Montague Maxwell Carpendale, son of Maxwell Carpendale (son-in-law):

Residence - Drogheda - September 13, 1882

Occupation - Major 2nd Scuide Horse - September 13, 1882

Maxwell Carpendale (father):

Occupation - Clergyman

John Eccles (father):

Occupation - Clergyman

Wedding Witnesses:

John Eccles & Charles Frizell

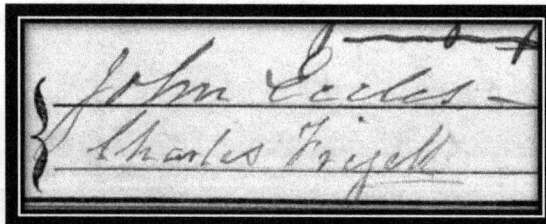

Signatures:

Eccles Surname Ireland: 1600s to 1900s

- Marion Jane Eccles & Frederick William Mervin – 3 Sep 1884 (Marriage, **Sandford Parish**)

Marion Jane Eccles (daughter):

   Residence - St. Peter's Rectory, Drogheda - September 3, 1884

Frederick William Mervin, son of William Hunter Mervin (son-in-law):

   Residence - 3 Sallymont Terrace, Ranelagh - September 3, 1884

   Occupation - Clerk in Holy Orders, B. A. - September 3, 1884

William Hunter Mervin (father):

   Occupation - Reverend

John Eccles (father):

   Occupation - Rector of St. Peter's, Drogheda

Wedding Witnesses:

John Eccles & A. W. Mervin

John Eccles (father):

   Occupation - Clergyman

               Rector of St. Peter's, Drogheda

John Eccles (son):

   Residence - Drogheda - August 2, 1854

   Occupation - Clerk in Holy Orders - August 2, 1854

Harriet Frizell, daughter of Charles Frizell (daughter-in-law):

   Residence - Wuington Place - August 2, 1854

Charles Frizell (father):

   Occupation - M D

Cuthbert Eccles (father):

   Occupation - Gentleman

Hurst

Wedding Witnesses:

Charles Frizell & Cuthbert Eccles

Signatures:

- Mary Anne Harriet Eccles – b. 14 Sep 1821, bapt. 17 Sep 1821 (Baptism, **St. George Parish**)

- Francis James Eccles – b. 16 Feb 1824, bapt. 5 Mar 1824 (Baptism, **St. George Parish**)

- Anthony Eccles – b. 31 May 1825, bapt. 20 Jun 1825 (Baptism, **St. George Parish**)

- Robert Eccles – bapt. 20 Jan 1827 (Baptism, **St. George Parish**)

- Hugh Eccles, b. 14 Feb 1828, bapt. 20 Feb 1828 (Baptism, **St. George Parish**) & Isabel Reid – 15 Mar 1866 (Marriage, **St. Stephen Parish**)

Signature:

Signatures (Marriage):

Hugh Eccles (son):

Residence - Northumberland Road - March 15, 1866

Occupation - Captain 56ᵗʰ Regiment - March 15, 1866

Isabel Reid, daughter of Alexander Reid (daughter-in-law):

Residence - 67 Pembroke Road - March 15, 1866

Eccles Surname Ireland: 1600s to 1900s

Alexander Reid (father):

Signature:

    Occupation - Esquire

Cuthbert Eccles (father):

    Occupation - Officer in the Army

Wedding Witnesses:

Alex Reid & Cuthbert Eccles

Signatures:

- o   Emily Eccles – b. 25 Aug 1829, bapt. 6 Sep 1829 (Baptism, **St. George Parish**)

- o   Harriet Eccles, b. 14 Jan 1831, bapt. 26 Jan 1831 (Baptism, **St. George Parish**) & John Crossby

    Seymour – 11 Oct 1877 (Marriage, **St. Peter Parish**)

Signatures:

Hurst

Harriet Eccles (daughter):

    Residence - 5 Clyde Road - October 11, 1877

John Crossby Seymour, son of John Crossby Seymour (son-in-law):

    Residence - Victoria House, Kingstown - October 11, 1877

    Occupation - Clerk in Holy Orders - October 11, 1877

    Relationship Status at Marriage - widow

John Crossby Seymour (father):

    Occupation - Clerk in Holy Orders

Cuthbert Eccles (father):

    Occupation - Gentleman

Wedding Witnesses:

Hugh Eccles & Edward Seymour

Signatures:

- o   Cuthbert Eccles – b. 1 May 1832, bapt. 12 May 1832 (Baptism, **St. George Parish**)

- o   Catherine Eccles – b. 22 Jul 1836, bapt. 18 Aug 1836 (Baptism, **St. George Parish**)

Cuthbert Eccles (father):

    Residence - No 93 Dorset Street, Co. Dublin - April 30, 1819

        Eccles Street - January 20, 1827

            February 20, 1828

            September 6, 1829

            January 26, 1831

            May 12, 1832

        No 43 Eccles Street - August 18, 1836

Occupation - Gentleman - January 20, 1827

February 20, 1828

Esquire - April 30, 1819

September 6, 1829

January 26, 1831

May 12, 1832

August 18, 1836

Wedding Witnesses:

L. H. Thomas, William Eccles, Thomas William Warren, and Edward O'Reilly

Signatures:

- George Eccles & Unknown

Signature:

  - o Anne Eccles (1st Marriage) & Unknown Edward

  - o Anne Eccles Edwards (2nd Marriage) & Joseph Parker – 14 Oct 1874 (Marriage, **St. Thomas Parish**)

Signatures:

Anne Eccles Edward (daughter):

  Residence - 64 Lower Sheriff Street - October 14, 1874

  Relationship Status at Marriage - widow

Joseph Parker, son of John Parker (son-in-law):

  Residence - 85 Anne Street - October 14, 1874

  Occupation - Bootmaker - October 14, 1874

  Relationship Status at Marriage - widow

John Parker (father):

  Occupation - Bootmaker

George Eccles (father):

  Occupation - Schoolmaster

Eccles Surname Ireland: 1600s to 1900s

Wedding Witnesses:

Henry Williams & George Eccles

Signatures:

- Gulielmo Eccles & Rebecca Eaton – 30 Apr 1797 (Marriage, **St. Andrew Parish (RC)**)

- Henry Eccles & Harriet Larry

  o Henry Eccles – b. 15 Aug 1878, bapt. 23 Aug 1878 (Baptism, **St. Nicholas Parish (RC)**)

Henry Eccles (father):

  Residence - Coombe Hospital - August 23, 1878

- Hugh Eccles & Annabelle Harrietta Unknown

  o Hugh Eccles – bapt. 10 Aug 1830 (Baptism, **St. Peter Parish**)

Hugh Eccles (father):

  Residence - Rathgar - August 10, 1830

- Hugh Eccles & Elizabeth Ambrose – 1 Sep 1735 (Marriage, **St. Mary Parish**)

  o Isaac Ambrose Eccles – b. 9 Jul 1736, bapt. 19 Jul 1736 (Baptism, **St. Mary Parish**)

  o John Eccles – b. 3 Nov 1738, bapt. 3 Dec 1738 (Baptism, **St. Mary Parish**)

  o Unknown Eccles – bapt. 1 Jan 1740 (Baptism, **St. Mary Parish**)

  o William Eccles – bapt. 9 Nov 1741 (Baptism, **St. Mary Parish**)

Hugh Eccles (father):

  Occupation - Esquire - January 1, 1740

  November 9, 1741

- Hugh Eccles & Mary Yarner (Y a r n e r) – 19 Dec 1693 (Marriage, **St. Michan Parish**)

Hugh Eccles (husband):

Occupation - Esquire - December 19, 1693

Mary Yarner (wife):

Relationship Status at Marriage - widow

- Hugh Eccles & Unknown

  o Elizabeth Eccles & Henry William Crosbie Ward – 8 Apr 1874 (Marriage, **St. Peter Parish**)

Signatures:

Elizabeth Eccles (daughter):

Residence - South Hill Cottage, Blackrock - April 8, 1874

Henry William Crosbie Ward, son of Edward Southwell (son-in-law):

Residence - 3 Alma Terrace, Monkstown - April 8, 1874

Occupation - Honorable Late Captain 43rd Regiment - April 8, 1874

Relationship Status at Marriage - widow

Edward Southwell (father):

Occupation - Viscount Banyan

Hugh Eccles (father):

Occupation - Esquire

Eccles Surname Ireland: 1600s to 1900s

- Isaac Ambrose Eccles & Unknown

    o Samuel Eccles & Catherine Sanigaer White – 15 Jun 1865 (Marriage, **St. Anne Parish**)

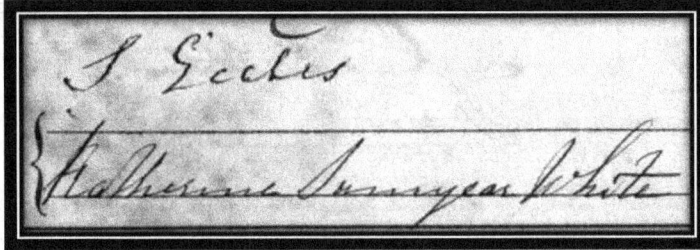

Signatures:

Samuel Eccles (son):

    Residence - Eccles Hall, Delgany - June 15, 1865

    Occupation - Incumbent of St. George's Chapel - June 15, 1865

    Relationship Status at Marriage - widow

Catherine Sanigaer White, daughter of Thomas Frederick Augustus White

(daughter-in-law):

    Residence - 10 South Frederick Street - June 15, 1865

Thomas Frederick Augustus White (father):

    Occupation - Professor of Music

Isaac Ambrose Eccles (father):

    Occupation - Esquire

- James Eccles & Alice Eccles

    o Mary Eccles – b. 9 Apr 1710, bapt. 12 Apr 1710 (Baptism, **St. John Parish**), bur. 8 Feb 1711 (Burial,

    St. John Parish)

James Eccles (father):

    Residence - Blind Key - April 12, 1710

    Occupation - Hatter - April 12, 1710

- James Eccles & Margaret Unknown

    o Gulielmo Eccles – bapt. 1781 (Baptism, **St. Andrew Parish (RC)**)

Hurst

- James Eccles & Unknown

  o Ellen Eccles & John Robertson – 21 Oct 1873 (Marriage, **St. Peter Parish**)

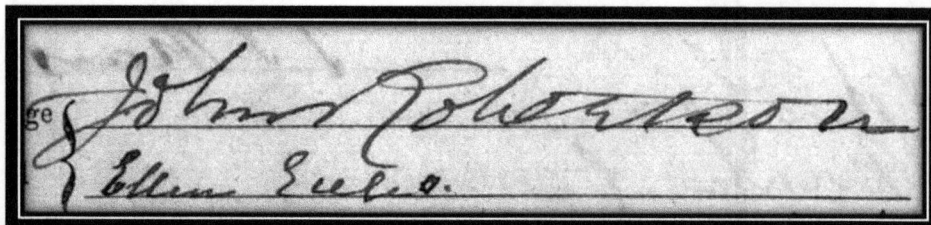

Signatures:

Ellen Eccles (daughter):

   Residence - 3 Charlemont Mall - October 21, 1873

John Robertson, son of Duncan Robertson (son-in-law):

   Residence - 13 Strandville Avenue, Clontarf - October 21, 1873

   Occupation - Commercial Traveller - October 21, 1873

Duncan Robertson (father):

   Occupation - Officer in the British Army

James Eccles (father):

   Occupation - Farmer

- John Eccles & Anne Mulligan

  o Joseph Eccles – b. 20 Sep 1886, bapt. 24 Sep 1886 (Baptism, **St. Michan Parish (RC)**)

John Eccles (father):

   Residence - 44 Beresford Street - September 24, 1886

- John Eccles & Eleanor Eccles

  o Jane Eccles – bapt. 15 Nov 1756 (Baptism, **St. Mark Parish**)

John Eccles (father):

   Residence - Sir John Rogerson's Quay - November 15, 1756

Eccles Surname Ireland: 1600s to 1900s

- John Eccles & Eleanor Eccles

  o John Henry Eccles – b. 22 Jul 1856, bapt. 9 Aug 1856 (Baptism, **St. Peter Parish**)

John Eccles (father):

  Residence - No 7 Long Lane - August 9, 1856

  Occupation - Law Clerk - August 9, 1856

- John Eccles & Eleanor Unknown

  o Sarah Eccles – bapt. 4 Dec 1777 (Baptism, **St. Michan Parish (RC)**)

- John Eccles (1st Marriage) & Elizabeth Eccles, bur. 18 Feb 1706 (Burial, **St. Mary Parish**)

  o John Eccles – bapt. 1 Oct 1695 (Baptism, **St. Michan Parish**), bur. 25 Mar 1699 (Burial, **St. Michan Parish**)

  o Jane Eccles – bapt. 29 Sep 1697 (Baptism, **St. Michan Parish**)

  o Richard Eccles – bur. 10 Apr 1698 (Burial, **St. Michan Parish**)

  o Anne Eccles – bapt. 9 Nov 1698 (Baptism, **St. Mary Parish**)

  o Margaret Eccles – bapt. 3 Feb 1700 (Baptism, **St. Mary Parish**)

  o John Eccles – bapt. 30 May 1701 (Baptism, **St. Mary Parish**)

  o Arabella Eccles – b. 5 Feb 1706, bapt. 10 Feb 1706 (Baptism, **St. Mary Parish**)

John Eccles (father):

  Occupation - Merchant - September 29, 1697

  November 9, 1698

  Alderman - May 30, 1701

  February 10, 1706

  Military Rank - Captain - October 1, 1695

- John Eccles (2nd Marriage) & Joyce Eccles, bur. 24 Oct 1709 (Burial, **St. Mary Parish**)

John Eccles (husband):

  Occupation - Alderman - October 24, 1709

Hurst

- John Eccles & Elizabeth Eccles

  o Henrietta Eccles – b. 3 Aug 1711, bapt. 20 Aug 1711 (Baptism, **St. John Parish**)

John Eccles (father):

Residence - Fishamble Street - August 20, 1711

Occupation - Gentleman - August 20, 1711

- John Eccles & Elizabeth Reilly

  o Joseph Eccles – b. 26 Oct 1873, bapt. 27 Oct 1873 (Baptism, **St. Michan Parish (RC)**)

John Eccles (father):

Residence - 55 Mary's Lane - October 27, 1873

- John Eccles & Margaret Campbell

  o Thomas Eccles & Mary Anne Forde – 30 Nov 1889 (Marriage, **St. Mary, Pro Cathedral Parish (RC)**)

Thomas Eccles (son):

Residence - 35 Mary's Lane - November 30, 1889

Mary Anne Forde, daughter of Michael Forde & Bridget Allen (daughter-in-law):

Residence - 37 Cole Lane - November 30, 1889

- John Eccles & Margaret Eccles

  o Margaret Eccles – bapt. 5 Apr 1828 (Baptism, **St. Mary, Pro Cathedral Parish (RC)**)

John Eccles (father):

Residence - Britain Street - April 5, 1828

- John Eccles & Margaret Eccles

  o Charles Eccles – bapt. 3 Feb 1837 (Baptism, **St. Mary Parish**)

John Eccles (father):

Residence - 9 Bolton Place - February 3, 1837

Occupation - Writing Clerk - February 3, 1837

Eccles Surname Ireland: 1600s to 1900s

- John Eccles & Margaret Eccles

  o Charles Eccles – bapt. 10 Feb 1837 (Baptism, **St. Mary, Pro Cathedral Parish (RC)**)

- John Eccles & Margaret Eccles

  o Elizabeth Catherine Eccles – b. 21 Oct 1857, bapt. 28 Oct 1857 (Baptism, **St. Michan Parish (RC)**)

John Eccles (father):

Residence - 10 Mary's Lane - October 28, 1857

- John Eccles & Margaret Eccles

  o Thomas Eccles & Alice Nolan – 23 Apr 1878 (Marriage, **St. Agatha Parish (RC)**) (Marriage, **St. Lawrence Parish (RC)**)

    ▪ John Joseph Eccles – b. 17 Aug 1880, bapt. 18 Aug 1880 (Baptism, **St. Mary, Pro Cathedral Parish (RC)**)

Thomas Eccles (son):

Residence - 28 Anne Street - April 23, 1878

22 Little Mary Street - August 18, 1880

Alice Nolan, daughter of Charles Nolan & Bridget Unknown (daughter-in-law):

Residence - 8 North William Street - April 23, 1878

- John Eccles & Margaret Matterson – 1 Oct 1820 (Marriage, **St. Paul Parish**)

- John Eccles & Margaret Unknown

  o John Eccles & Anne Reilly – 24 Jul 1859 (Marriage, **St. Michan Parish (RC)**)

    ▪ Joseph Eccles – b. 13 Feb 1866, bapt. 28 Feb 1866 (Baptism, **St. Michan Parish (RC)**)

    ▪ Joseph Eccles – b. 29 Aug 1868, bapt. 7 Sep 1868 (Baptism, **St. Michan Parish (RC)**)

    ▪ Margaret Eccles – b. 4 Jan 1876, bapt. 7 Jan 1876 (Baptism, **St. Michan Parish (RC)**)

    ▪ Thomas Eccles – b. 7 Jul 1878, bapt. 8 Jul 1878 (Baptism, **St. Michan Parish (RC)**)

Hurst

John Eccles (son):

Residence - 19 Boot Lane - July 24, 1859

27 Mary's Lane - February 28, 1866

2 Beresford Street - September 7, 1868

35 Mary's Lane - January 7, 1876

July 8, 1878

Anne Reilly, daughter of John Reilly & Mary Unknown (daughter-in-law):

Residence - 28 Mary's Lane - July 24, 1859

- John Eccles & Mary Eccles

  o Mary Eccles – bapt. 1 Mar 1766 (Baptism, **St. Mark Parish**)

John Eccles (father):

Residence - Rings End - March 1, 1766

- John Eccles & Mary Murphy

  o Elizabeth Eccles – b. 27 Nov 1850, bapt. 27 Nov 1850 (Baptism, **Glengarriff Parish (RC)**)

  o Ellen Eccles – b. 17 Oct 1852, bapt. 17 Oct 1852 (Baptism, **Glengarriff Parish (RC)**)

John Eccles (father):

Residence - Reenmeen - November 27, 1850

October 17, 1852

- John Eccles & Mary O'Brien

  o Mary Eccles – b. 1859, bapt. 1859 (Baptism, **St. Andrew Parish (RC)**)

John Eccles (father):

Residence - Trinity Street - 1859

- John Eccles & Sarah Middlebrook – 13 Aug 1724 (Marriage, **St. John Parish**)

Eccles Surname Ireland: 1600s to 1900s

- John Eccles & Unknown

  o Jeremiah Eccles – bur. 22 Jan 1704 (Burial, **St. Werburgh Parish**)

Jeremiah Eccles (son):

    Age at Death -infant

    Place of Burial - Churchyard

- John Eccles & Unknown

  o John Eccles & Eleanor Burns (B u r n s) – 12 Dec 1849 (Marriage, **St. Thomas Parish**)

Signatures:

John Eccles (son):

    Residence - Castle Rurck - December 12, 1849

    Occupation - Clerk - December 12, 1849

Eleanor Burns, daughter of Henry Burns (daughter-in-law):

    Residence - 3 Annesley Place - December 12, 1849

Henry Burns (father):

    Occupation - Shopkeeper

John Eccles (father):

    Occupation - Hotel Keeper

Wedding Witnesses:

William Burns & Michael Power

Signatures:

- John Eccles & Unknown

  o Samuel Eccles & Catherine Cahill – 9 Jun 1852 (Marriage, **St. Peter Parish**)

Signatures:

  ▪ Elizabeth Mary Eccles – bapt. 3 Dec 1852 (Baptism, **St. Nicholas Parish (RC)**)

  ▪ John Lawrence Eccles – b. 13 Apr 1855, bapt. 13 May 1855 (Baptism, **St. Peter Parish**) (Baptism,

   SS. Michael & John Parish (RC))

Samuel Eccles (son):

   Residence - 44 Aungier Street - June 9, 1852

                45 Aungier Street - May 13, 1855

   Occupation - Watch Maker - June 9, 1852

                Cloth Maker - May 13, 1855

   Relationship Status at Marriage - minor

Catherine Cahill, daughter of Lawrence Cahill (daughter-in-law):

   Residence - 45 Aungier Street - June 9, 1852

Eccles Surname Ireland: 1600s to 1900s

Lawrence Cahill (father):

Occupation - Baker

John Eccles (father):

Occupation - Writing Clerk

- John Dickson Eccles & Unknown

  o Elizabeth Mary Frances Wilhelmina Eccles & Benjamin Arthur Newcombe – 28 Oct 1852 (Marriage, **St.** Peter Parish)

Signatures:

Elizabeth Mary France Wilhelmina Eccles (daughter):

Residence - 33 Pembroke Place - October 28, 1852

Benjamin Arthur Newcombe, son of William Newcombe (son-in-law):

Residence - Carland, Dungannon - October 28, 1852

Occupation - Clerk in Holy Orders - October 28, 1852

William Newcombe (father):

Occupation - Merchant

John Dickson Eccles (father):

Occupation - Esquire

Wedding Witnesses:

William Newcombe & William W. Vickers

Signatures:

Hurst

- John Philip Eccles & Isabel O'Gorman (O 'G o r m a n)

    o John Patrick Eccles & Alice Baker – 10 Oct 1903 (Marriage, **St. Mary, Pro Cathedral Parish (RC)**)

John Patrick Eccles (son):

Residence - 16 Lower Columbia Road - October 10, 1903

Alice Baker, daughter of William Baker & Margaret Mooney (daughter-in-law):

Residence - 38 Hardwick Street - October 10, 1903

Wedding Witnesses:

Timothy Eccles & Eveline Baker

    o Alice Eccles – b. 1 Apr 1873, bapt. 7 Apr 1873 (Baptism, **St. Mary, Pro Cathedral Parish (RC)**)

    o Edward Thomas Eccles – b. 10 Sep 1875, bapt. 27 Sep 1875 (Baptism, **St. Lawrence Parish (RC)**)

John Eccles (father):

Residence - 37 Sumner Street - April 7, 1873

10 Marshall Terrace, North Strand - September 27, 1875

- Jonathan Eccles & Mary Unknown

    o Samuel Eccles – bapt. 4 Mar 1769 (Baptism, **St. Peter Parish**)

- Lawrence Eccles & Unknown

    o Richard Eccles – bur. 28 Aug 1669 (Burial, **St. John Parish**)

- Michael Eccles & Mary A. Reilly

    o Emily Eccles & Dominick Fitzmaurice – 9 Aug 1903 (Marriage, **St. Mary, Pro Cathedral Parish (RC)**)

Emily Eccles (daughter):

Residence - 13 Rotunda Market - August 9, 1903

Dominick Fitzmaurice, son of Dominick Fitzmaurice & Elizabeth Young (son-in-law):

Residence - 14 Rotunda Market - August 9, 1903

Eccles Surname Ireland: 1600s to 1900s

- Owen Eccles & Anne Unknown

    o Mary Eccles – bapt. 17 Jun 1750 (Baptism, **St. Michan Parish (RC)**)

- Patrick Eccles & Catherine Cullen

    o John Eccles – b. 22 May 1885, bapt. 1 Jun 1885 (Baptism, **St. Michan Parish (RC)**)

    o Peter Eccles – b. 16 Jun 1887, bapt. 27 Jun 1887 (Baptism, **St. Michan Parish (RC)**)

Patrick Eccles (father):

Residence - 34 Church Street - June 1, 1885

35 Mary's Lane - June 27, 1887

- Patrick Eccles & Ellen Derie

    o Michael Eccles – bapt. 22 Oct 1816 (Baptism, **Rossalettiri & Kilkeraunmor (Roscarbery & Lissevard) Parish (RC)**)

- Richard Eccles & Catherine Donovan

    o Mary Eccles – bapt. 15 Sep 1830 (Baptism, **Rossalettiri & Kilkeraunmor (Roscarbery & Lissevard) Parish (RC)**)

    o Timothy Eccles – bapt. 1 Feb 1837 (Baptism, **Rossalettiri & Kilkeraunmor (Roscarbery & Lissevard) Parish (RC)**)

Richard Eccles (father):

Residence - Ross - February 1, 1837

- Richard Eccles & Margaret Unknown

    o Mary Frances Eccles – b. 1858, bapt. 1858 (Baptism, **St. Andrew Parish (RC)**)

- Robert Eccles & Anne Eccles

    o William Eccles – b. 2 Dec 1724, bapt. 6 Dec 1724 (Baptism, **St. Mary Parish**)

Hurst

- Robert Eccles & Anne Halpin

    o Robert Patrick Eccles – b. 20 Aug 1859, bapt. 31 Aug 1859 (Baptism, **St. Mary, Pro Cathedral Parish (RC)**)

    o Dennis Eccles – b. 19 Jul 1862, bapt. 31 Jul 1862 (Baptism, **St. James Parish (RC)**)

Robert Eccles (father):

Residence - 10 Temple Street - August 31, 1859

Rutland Avenue - July 31, 1862

- Robert Eccles & Elizabeth Eccles, bur. 21 Nov 1718 (Burial, **St. Mary Parish**)

Elizabeth Eccles (wife):

Social Status - poor

- Robert Eccles & Frances White – 12 Apr 1829 (Marriage, **St. Audoen Parish**)

Signatures:

    o Charles Eccles – bapt. 3 May 1830 (Baptism, **St. Audoen Parish (RC)**)

Robert Eccles (father):

Residence - Dunlavin Parish - April 12, 1829

Frances White (mother):

Residence - St. Audoen Parish - April 12, 1829

Eccles Surname Ireland: 1600s to 1900s

Wedding Witnesses:

John Stokes & Richard White

Signatures:

- Robert Eccles & Mary Smith

  o Margaret Eccles & Jeremiah Hogan – 25 Sep 1894 (Marriage, **St. Mary, Pro Cathedral Parish**

    (RC))

Margaret Eccles (daughter):

Residence - **25 Temple Street - September 25, 1894**

Jeremiah Hogan, son of John Hogan & Anne Vaughn (son-in-law):

Residence - **46 Arranmore Terrace - September 25, 1894**

- Robert Eccles & Unknown

  o Mary Hannah Eccles & Alfred James Walter – 29 Apr 1880 (Marriage, **St. Paul Parish**)

Signatures:

Mary Hannah Eccles (daughter):

    Residence - Royal Barracks - April 29, 1880

    Relationship Status at Marriage - minor

Alfred James Walter, son of James Walter (son-in-law):

    Residence - Royal Barracks - April 29, 1880

    Occupation - Color Sergeant 57th Foot - April 29, 1880

James Walter (father):

    Occupation - Clerk

Robert Eccles (father):

    Occupation - Agent

Wedding Witnesses:

Jesse Eccles & Alicia Victoria Street

Signatures:

Eccles Surname Ireland: 1600s to 1900s

- Samuel Eccles & Catherine Eccles

  o Jane Eccles – bapt. 19 Oct 1851 (Baptism, **Skibbereen (Creagh & Sullon) Parish (RC)**)

Samuel Eccles (father):

Residence - High Street - October 19, 1851

- Samuel Eccles & Catherine Harrington

  o William Eccles – bapt. 20 Mar 1838 (Baptism, **Skibbereen (Creagh & Sullon) Parish (RC)**)

  o John Eccles – bapt. 3 Mar 1840 (Baptism, **Bantry Parish (RC)**)

  o Charlotte Eccles – bapt. 10 Sep 1842 (Baptism, **Bantry Parish (RC)**)

- Samuel Eccles & Frances Eccles

  o Robert Eccles & Anne McTigh – 6 Jun 1858 (Marriage, **St. Mary, Pro Cathedral Parish (RC)**)

Robert Eccles (son):

Residence - 13 Upper Dorset Street - June 6, 1858

Anne McTigh, daughter of Bernard McTigh & Bridget McTigh (daughter-in-law):

Residence - 61 Mountjoy Street - June 6, 1858

- Samuel Eccles & Sarah Unknown

  o Sarah Louisa Eccles – b. 2 Oct 1878, bapt. 27 Oct 1878 (Baptism, **St. James Parish**)

Samuel Eccles (father):

Residence - 1 Connaught Terrace - October 27, 1878

Occupation - Writing Clerk - October 27, 1878

- Thomas Eccles & Jane Eccles

  o Thomas Eccles – bapt, 11 Jun 1783 (Baptism, **St. Mary Parish**)

- Thomas Eccles & Mary Eccles

  o Mary Eccles – b. 3 Dec 1716, bapt. 17 Dec 1716 (Baptism, **St. Mary Parish**), bur. 2 Oct 1721 (Burial,

    St. Mary Parish)

  o John Eccles – bapt. 21 Sep 1718 (Baptism, **St. Mary Parish**)

  o Thomas Eccles – b. 10 Aug 1721, bapt. 25 Aug 1721 (Baptism, **St. Mary Parish**)

  o William Eccles – bur. 11 Jun 1726 (Burial, **St. Mary Parish**)

Thomas Eccles (father):

Occupation - Gentleman - December 17, 1716

- Thomas Eccles & Mary Unknown

  o Elizabeth Charlotte Bridget Eccles – bapt. 25 Jan 1768 (Baptism, **St. Michan Parish (RC)**)

  o Teresa Eccles – bapt. 30 Dec 1773 (Baptism, **St. Michan Parish (RC)**)

- Thomas Eccles & Unknown

  o Henry Richard Eccles & Alice Hawkin – 4 Aug 1890 (Marriage, **St. Thomas Parish**)

Signature:

Signatures (Marriage):

Eccles Surname Ireland: 1600s to 1900s

Henry R. Eccles (son):

Residence - 59 North Strand Road - August 4, 1890

Occupation - Pressman - August 4, 1890

Relationship Status at Marriage - widow

Alice Hawkin, daughter of Frederick T. Hawkin (daughter-in-law):

Residence - 59 North Strand Road - August 4, 1890

Frederick T. Hawkin (father):

Occupation - Clerk Church of Ireland

Thomas Eccles (father):

Occupation - Gentleman

- Unknown Eccles & Unknown Simon – 17 Oct 1767 (Marriage, **St. Mary Parish**)

Unknown Simon (wife):

Residence - Jervis Quay - October 17, 1767

- William Eccles & Anne Eccles

  o Sarah Eccles – bapt. 13 Apr 1729 (Baptism, **St. Mary Parish**)

- William Eccles & Catherine Unknown

  o Jane Catherine Eccles – bapt. 12 Apr 1833 (Baptism, **St. Mary, Pro Cathedral Parish (RC)**)

- William Eccles & Mary Lehane

  o Mary Eccles – bapt. 7 Mar 1845 (Baptism, **Bantry Parish (RC)**)

- William Eccles & Sarah Smith – 18 Feb 1817 (Marriage, **St. Peter Parish**)

William Eccles (husband):

Residence - Kithimon, Co. Wicklow - February 18, 1817

Sarah Smith (wife):

Residence - St. Peter Parish - February 18, 1817

Wedding Witnesses:

Hugh Eccles & William Smith

Hurst

- William Eccles & Susan Eccles

  o Mary Eccles – b. 5 Jan 1811, bapt. 12 Apr 1811 (Baptism, **St. George Parish**)

  o Frances Eccles – b. 8 May 1813, bapt. 13 Jun 1813 (Baptism, **St. George Parish**)

  o Charlotte Eccles – b. 4 Dec 1816, bapt. 3 Feb 1817 (Baptism, **St. George Parish**)

- William George Eccles & Mary Anne Unknown

  o John Cromwell Eccles – bapt. 14 Jun 1805 (Baptism, **St. Audoen Parish**)

Individual Births/Baptisms

- Alice Eccles – bapt. 31 Mar 1711 (Baptism, **St. John Parish**)

- Elizabeth Eccles – b. 1 Mar 1839, bapt. 13 Mar 1839 (Baptism, **St. George Parish**)

Elizabeth Eccles (child):

  Remarks at Birth - foundling

- Ellen Eccles – b. 23 Feb 1848, bapt. 27 Feb 1848 (Baptism, **St. George Parish**)

Ellen Eccles (child):

  Remarks - found on Eccles Street

  Remarks at Birth - foundling

- Hugh Eccles – bapt. 31 Mar 1711 (Baptism, **St. Patrick Parish**)

- Mary Eccles – bapt. Unclear (Baptism, **St. Michan Parish (RC)**)

Mary Eccles (child):

  Residence - Lower Eccles Lane - Unclear

Individual Burials

- Anne Eccles – bur. 2 Dec 1679 (Burial, **St. Catherine Parish**)

- Catherine Eccles – b. May 1866, bur. 17 Nov 1866 (Burial, **St. George Parish**)

Catherine Eccles (deceased):

    Residence - 33 Cumberland Street - Before November 17, 1866

    Age at Death - 7 months

- Charles Eccles – bur. 19 Feb 1761 (Burial, **St. Mary Parish**)

Charles Eccles (deceased):

    Residence - Mary Street - Before February 19, 1761

- E. Eccles – b. 1833, bur. 4 Nov 1834 (Burial, **St. George Parish**)

E. Eccles (deceased):

    Residence - Eccles Lane - Before November 4, 1834

    Age at Death - 1 year

- Elford Eccles – bur. 17 Dec 1821 (Burial, **St. Nicholas Without Parish**)

Elford Eccles (deceased):

    Residence - 15 South George's Street - Before December 17, 1821

- Elizabeth Eccles – bur. 3 Jan 1680 (Burial, **St. John Parish**)

- Elizabeth Eccles – bur. 6 Jun 1753 (Burial, **St. John Parish**)

- Elizabeth Eccles – bur. 22 Nov 1771 (Burial, **St. Peter Parish**)

- Elizabeth Eccles – bur. 11 Jan 1805 (Burial, **St. Paul Parish**)

- Elizabeth Eccles – b. Mar 1839, bur. 13 Aug 1839 (Burial, **St. George Parish**)

Elizabeth Eccles (deceased):

    Residence - Whites Lane - Before August 13, 1839

    Age at Death - 6 months

Eccles Surname Ireland: 1600s to 1900s

- Henry Eccles – bur. 2 Apr 1818 (Burial, **St. John Parish**)

- Hugh Eccles – bur. 16 Oct 1716 (Burial, **St. Mary Parish**)

Hugh Eccles (deceased):

> **Military Rank - Captain - October 16, 1716**

- James Eccles – bur. 10 Aug 1725 (Burial, **St. John Parish**)

- James Eccles – bur. 23 Jan 1727 (Burial, **St. Mary Parish**)

- James Eccles – bur. 16 Dec 1773 (Burial, **St. Paul Parish**)

James Eccles (deceased):

> **Residence - The Bachelor's Walk - Before December 16, 1773**

- James Eccles – bur. 25 Dec 1777 (Burial, **St. James Parish**)

James Eccles (deceased):

> **Residence - Bridge Street - Before December 25, 1777**

- Jane Eccles – bur. 7 Dec 1787 (Burial, **St. Paul Parish**)

- John Eccles – bur. 20 Jan 1675 (Burial, **St. John Parish**)

- John Eccles – bur. 9 Mar 1777 (Burial, **St. Mark Parish**)

- John Eccles – b. Dec 1841, bur. 3 Feb 1842 (Burial, **St. Paul Parish**)

John Eccles (deceased):

> **Residence - Island Bridge - Before February 3, 1842**
>
> **Age at Death - 3 months**

- Joseph Eccles – bur. 3 Mar 1717 (Burial, **St. Mary Parish**)

- Lydia Eccles – bur. 28 Apr 1767 (Burial, **St. Peter Parish**)

- Margaret Eccles – b. 1782, d. 16 Oct 1824, bur. 1824 (Burial, **St. Peter Parish**)

Margaret Eccles (deceased):

> **Residence - Johnson Place, St. Anne Parish - October 16, 1824**

Hurst

- Mary Eccles – bur. 18 Apr 1702 (Burial, **St. Nicholas Without Parish**)

Mary Eccles (deceased):

   Remarks about Burial - buried in Mr. Linager's vault

- Mary Eccles – bur. 18 Apr 1725 (Burial, **St. Mary Parish**)

- Mary Eccles – bur. Oct 1734 (Burial, **St. Nicholas Without Parish**)

Mary Eccles (deceased):

   Residence - Francis Street - October 1734

- Mary Eccles – bur. 16 Jul 1762 (Burial, **St. Peter Parish**)

- Mary Eccles – b. 1763, bur. 27 Jun 1825 (Burial, **St. Mary Parish**)

Mary Eccles (deceased):

   Residence - St. Andrew Parish - Before June 27, 1825

   Age at Death - 62 years

- Sarah Eccles (Child) – bur. 9 Aug 1731 (Burial, **St. Paul Parish**)

- Thomas Eccles – bur. 5 Mar 1709 (Burial, **St. Nicholas Within Parish**)

- Unknown Eccles – bur. 11 Mar 1755 (Burial, **St. John Parish**)

- Unknown Eccles, Mrs. – bur. 2 May 1796 (Burial, **St. Mary Parish**)

Unknown Eccles, Mrs. (deceased):

   Residence - Bolton Street - Before May 2, 1796

- William Eccles – b. Oct 1716, bur. 7 Jan 1817 (Burial, **St. Mark Parish**)

William Eccles (deceased):

   Age at Death - 3 months

Individual Marriages

- Alice Eccles & Edward Lyons – 1 Jun 1850 (Marriage, St. Mary, Pro Cathedral Parish (RC))

- Anne Eccles & James Kinane (K i n a n e) – 30 Jul 1786 (Marriage, St. Michan Parish (RC))

- Elizabeth L. S. Eccles & William Newcomb – 23 Oct 1813 (Marriage, St. George Parish)

William Newcomb (husband):

    Occupation - Esquire - October 23, 1813

- Ellen Eccles & Peter Gaffney

    o   Peter Gaffney – b. 25 May 1854, bapt. 29 May 1854 (Baptism, St. Mary, Pro Cathedral Parish

        (RC))

Peter Gaffney (father):

    Residence - 5 Green Street - May 29, 1854

- Esther Eccles & Patrick McDonald

    o   James McDonald – bapt. 2 Jan 1832 (Baptism, St. Michan Parish (RC))

- Frances Eccles & Charles Lucas – 27 Jul 1811 (Marriage, St. George Parish)

Charles Lucas (husband):

    Occupation - Captain, Fermaugh - July 27, 1811

- Jane Eccles & James Baird – 22 Feb 1789 (Marriage, St. Mary Parish)

James Baird (husband):

    Occupation - Gentleman - February 22, 1789

- Jane Eccles & Patrick Lawlor – 16 Feb 1871 (Marriage, **Cork - SS. Peter & Paul Parish (RC)**)

  o Mary Jane Lawlor – b. 3 Jun 1875, bapt. 13 Jun 1875 (Baptism, **St. Michan Parish (RC)**)

Jane Eccles (mother):

Residence - 123 Old George Street - February 16, 1871

Patrick Lawlor (father):

Residence - Garften Alley - February 16, 1871

Binns Bridge Cottage - June 13, 1875

- Jane Eccles & William Cregin – 15 Nov 1836 (Marriage, **St. George Parish**)

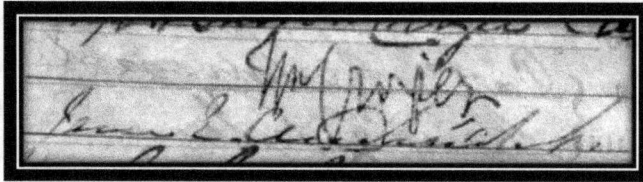

Signatures:

William Cregin (husband):

Residence - Enniskillen - November 15, 1836

Occupation - Esquire - November 15, 1836

- Joan Eccles & John Foreman

  o Mary Anne Alam Foreman – bapt. 16 Apr 1832 (Baptism, **St. Michan Parish (RC)**)

- Joan Eccles & Michael Regan

  o Joan Regan – bapt. 10 Apr 1844 (Baptism, **Rossalettiri & Kilkeraunmor (Roscarbery & Lissevard) Parish (RC)**)

Michael Regan (father):

Residence - Carrigfada - April 10, 1844

Eccles Surname Ireland: 1600s to 1900s

- Margaret Eccles & Richard Smith – 29 Jul 1855 (Marriage, **St. Andrew Parish** (RC))

  o Joseph John Smith – bapt. 1856 (Baptism, **St. Andrew Parish** (RC))

  o Margaret Catherine Smith – b. 1860, bapt. 1860 (Baptism, **St. Andrew Parish** (RC))

Richard Smith (father):

Residence - 4 Coppinger's Row - 1860

- Mary Eccles & Edward Reilly

  o Esther Reilly – bapt. 1849 (Baptism, **Saggart Parish** (RC))

- Mary Anne Eccles & James Mahon – 21 Apr 1856 (Marriage, **St. Mary, Pro Cathedral Parish** (RC))

- Sarah Eccles & Robert Joulyn Phillips – 16 Jun 1815 (Marriage, **St. George Parish**)

- Susan Eccles & Richard Smith – 9 May 1682 (Marriage, **St. Michael Parish**)

Name Variations

Includes Latin and Abbreviated forms of names found in the original documents.

Abigail = Abigale, Abigall

Anne = Ann, Anna, Annae

Bartholomew = Barth, Bartholmeus, Bartholomeo

Bridget = Birgis, Brigid, Brigida, Bridgit

Catherine = Catharine, Catharina, Catharinae, Catherina, Cath, Catha, Cathae, Cathe, Cathn, Kate

Charles = Carolus, Charls, Chas

Christopher = Christoph

Daniel = Danielem, Danielis

Edmund = Edmond

Edward = Ed, Edwd

Eleanor = Eleo, Eleonora, Elinor, Ellenor

Elizabeth = Betty, Elisa, Elisabeth, Eliz, Eliza, Elizab, Elizh, Elizth

Ellen = Elena, Ellena

Esther = Essie, Ester

Francis = Fransicum

George = Geo, Georg, Georgius

Grace = Gratiae

Gulielmo = Guil, Guillelmi, Gulielmum, Guillelmus, Gulmi

Harold = Harry

Helen = Helena

Eccles Surname Ireland: 1600s to 1900s

Honor = Hanora, Honora

Hugh = Hew

James = Jacobi, Jacobus, Jas

Jane = Joanna

Jeanne = Jeannae, Joannae

Joan = Johanna, Joney

John = Jno, Joannem, Joannes, Johannis

Joseph = Jos

Juliana = Julian

Leticia = Letitia, Lettice, Letticia

Margaret = Margarita, Margaritae, Margeret, Marget, Margt

Martha = Marthae

Mary = Maria, My

Mary Anne = Marianna, Marianne, Maryanne

Michael = Michaelis, Michl

Patrick = Pat, Patt, Patk, Patricii, Patricius

Peter = Petri

Richard = Ricardi, Ricardus, Rich, Richd

Robert = Roberti

Rose = Rosa, Rosae

Samuel = Samuelis

Thomas = Thom, Thomae, Thoms, Thos, Ths

Timothy = Timotheus, Timy

Valentine = Val, Valentinae, Valentinus

William = Wil, Will, Willm, Wm

Notes

Notes

Notes

Notes

Notes

Notes

Index

Eccles Surname Ireland: 1600s to 1900s

Eccles Surname Ireland: 1600s to 1900s

V

Vaughan

W

Walter

Ward

White

Y

Yarner

Young

About The Author

Donovan Hurst graduated from San Diego State University with a Bachelor of Arts in the major field of studies of History and a minor in the field of studies of Anthropology. He is a current member of The General Society of Mayflower Descendants and has been conducting genealogical research for over 10 years tracing back his ancestors to their ancestral homelands in Denmark, England, France, Germany, Ireland, Norway, and Scotland.